WHAT ON EARTH?
Climate Change Explained

T0011272

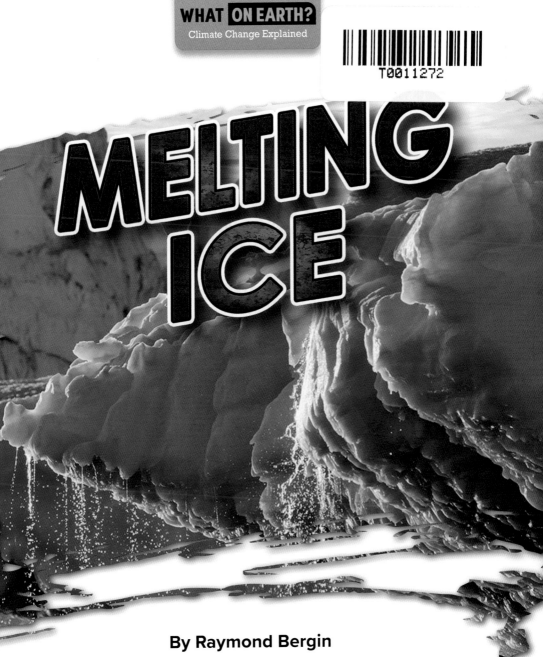

MELTING ICE

By Raymond Bergin

Consultant: David L. Fox
Professor of Earth & Environmental Sciences
University of Minnesota

BEARPORT
PUBLISHING

Minneapolis, Minnesota

Credits

Cover and title page, © Paul Souders/Getty, © djgis/Shutterstock; 4–5,
© imageBROKER/Alamy; 6–7, © shaunl/iStockphoto; 8–9, © Ashley Cooper/Getty;
10–11, © VisualCommunications/iStockphoto; 12, © Subodh Agnihotri/iStockphoto;
13, © posteriori/iStockphoto; 14–15, © Prisma by Dukas Presseagentur GmbH /Alamy;
16–17, © Joe Raedle/Getty; 18–19, © gdagys/iStockphoto; 21, © nadtochiy/Shutterstock;
24–25, © narvikk/iStockphoto; 26–27, © Ashley Cooper/Getty; 28, © Michal Balada/
iStockphoto; 29, © Toa55/iStockphoto; , © JohnnyGreig/iStockphoto; , © aluxum/
iStockphoto; , © LeoPatrizi/iStockphoto; , © inakiantonana/iStockphoto.

President: Jen Jenson
Director of Product Development: Spencer Brinker
Senior Editor: Allison Juda
Associate Editor: Charly Haley
Senior Designer: Colin O'Dea

Library of Congress Cataloging-in-Publication Data

Names: Bergin, Raymond, 1968- author.
Title: Melting ice / by Raymond Bergin.
Description: Minneapolis, Minnesota : Bearport Publishing Company, [2022] |
  Series: What on earth? climate change explained | Includes
  bibliographical references and index.
Identifiers: LCCN 2021039162 (print) | LCCN 2021039163 (ebook) | ISBN
  9781636915579 (library binding) | ISBN 9781636915647 (paperback) | ISBN
  9781636915715 (ebook)
Subjects: LCSH: Climatic changes--Juvenile literature. | Sea ice--Juvenile
  literature.
Classification: LCC QC903.15 .B47 2022 (print) | LCC QC903.15 (ebook) |
  DDC 551.31--dc23
LC record available at https://lccn.loc.gov/2021039162
LC ebook record available at https://lccn.loc.gov/2021039163

For more information, write to Bearport Publishing, 5357 Penn Avenue South, Minneapolis,
MN 55419. Printed in the United States of America

Contents

The Birth of an Iceberg

A wall of ice towers high above **frigid** ocean water. Suddenly, a series of sharp cracks thunder across the sea, followed by a loud boom. Frozen chunks begin to tumble into the water. And then a huge slab of ice taller than three Empire State Buildings breaks away from the wall and roars down into the ocean. Its splash sends out gigantic waves.

A warming planet and melting ice have created this huge iceberg. What on Earth is happening?

In 2021, an iceberg larger than the state of Rhode Island broke free from Antarctica. This chunk of ice was 105 miles (170 km) long and 15 miles (25 km) wide!

A Warming Planet

Our planet is warming quickly, and it's because of humans. When we burn **fossil fuels** to power our cars, homes, and factories, gases such as **carbon dioxide** are released into the **atmosphere**. These gases form a kind of blanket that traps heat around the planet.

The extra heat in Earth's atmosphere is causing the air and ocean to warm up. It is changing our **climate**, or the usual weather in an area. Even our planet's coldest, iciest spots—the Arctic and the Antarctic—are getting warmer.

The entire world is heating up, but it is especially a problem at the poles. The Arctic in the north is warming twice as fast as the global average. The South Pole in the center of Antarctica is warming three times as fast.

Factories are big contributors to the fossil fuels in our atmosphere.

Endangered Ice

Glaciers are huge, thick pieces of ice that form on land. They are made from snow that was packed down over time into hard ice. Glaciers larger than 19,000 square miles (50,000 sq km) and that form on level land are called **ice sheets** or continental glaciers. Nearly all of our planet's glacial ice is found in two huge ice sheets that cover most of Greenland and Antarctica. There's a lot of ice, but much of it is in danger of melting because of higher air and ocean temperatures.

The Greenland Ice Sheet is 10,000 feet (3,000 m) thick—as tall as 33 Statues of Liberty stacked on top of one another! The Antarctic sheet is 15,000 ft (4,600 m) thick, or about 50 statues.

Weakening Walls of Ice

All this ice doesn't melt at once. First, sunlight and warm air melt the ice on the top. This warmed-up **meltwater** makes holes in the ice. It trickles down all the way to the rock beneath the glacier or ice sheet, cracking and weakening the ice as it goes.

When the trickling water reaches the bottom of the ice, it melts the edges of the huge blocks of ice, too. Eventually, the ice becomes weak enough that chunks of it break off and fall into the ocean.

Each year, the Greenland Ice Sheet dumps about 309 billion tons (280 billion t) of melting ice into the ocean. That could fill about 75,000 Olympic-sized swimming pools!

Losing Its Cool

It seems normal for ice to melt, but too much melting can cause some major problems for Earth. Ice keeps our planet from getting too hot. Its bright surface acts as a giant reflector, bouncing light and heat from the sun back into space.

When ice disappears, it uncovers the darker surfaces of seawater and soil. These darker areas **absorb** the light and heat, causing the water, ground, and air to warm. The added warmth melts even more ice, revealing more heat-absorbing dark surfaces. In this way, the cycle repeats and picks up speed.

During the cold months, sea ice forms in the ocean waters of the Arctic and Antarctic. But because of warmer winters, less sea ice has been forming. It has also been melting earlier as things heat up quicker in the spring.

An Overflowing Glass

Ice is also important because it holds water that would otherwise cover large parts of the land we live on. But as glaciers melt and break apart, **sea levels** rise and water moves farther onto land.

The icebergs and glacial meltwater that enter the ocean behave like ice cubes and water being added to a glass. When we add to the glass, the water level already there rises. The more we add, the higher the water level goes . . . and the more likely it is that the glass—or shorelines—will overflow.

Because of rising temperatures, the Greenland Ice Sheet is melting faster than ever. If it were to melt completely, the global sea level would rise by about 23 ft (7 m).

Melting Ice, Rising Water

Our global glass of ice water is already beginning to overflow! Since 1880, global sea levels have risen 8 to 9 inches (20 to 23 cm). Most experts expect the levels to continue to rise at least another foot (30 cm) by 2100.

Coastal cities are already seeing flooding at **high tide**, or the time of day when ocean water moves farthest onto land. Some islands in the Pacific Ocean have even disappeared under the higher seas. Several coastal and island communities have relocated or are planning to move to escape rising waters.

Some scientists think sea levels will rise even higher—as much as 8 ft (2.4 m) by 2100! This would put large cities, including Miami, Houston, and New Orleans, underwater.

High-tide flooding will only get worse if we don't stop climate change.

Stormy Seas

Coastal flooding can get even worse when huge ocean storms, such as hurricanes, hit land. And once again, melting ice is partly to blame.

When ocean storms rage, high winds create very tall waves. The taller the waves and the more powerful the winds pushing them forward, the farther onshore the water will travel. This can cause massive damage to towns and cities. Ocean water and wind can destroy homes and businesses, wash out roads, ruin crops, and take lives.

High waters forced some trapped residents in Thailand to escape flooding by paddling down streets on a makeshift raft.

Sea ice along the coastlines of Canada and Alaska helps block waves and winds that **erode** land. With more of this ice melting and less forming, these coastal communities are losing more land and having more floods.

Winds Take a Wrong Turn

Monster storms flooding coastal communities are just one example of the wild weather influenced by a warming planet and melting ice. The climate change is shifting the world's winds, too.

The difference in temperature between the Arctic and areas farther south creates powerful winds that circle the Arctic. These winds—called the polar jet stream—separate the cold in the north from the warmer weather of the south. But when Arctic ice melts, there is a smaller difference in temperature between the two areas. This makes the polar jet stream slow down and begin to wobble off course.

When there is a wobble in the jet stream, unusual warmth can pour into the Arctic and cause extreme melting. Meanwhile, frigid cold can shoot much farther south than normal.

Current Events

Melting ice is also affecting the way ocean water moves. Polar water is cold and salty. This makes it heavy, so it sinks. Warmer salty water moves in to replace the sinking water. As this water cools, it sinks, too. The sinking cycle creates **currents**. The movement of warm water to colder parts of the world evens out temperatures and makes much of our planet livable for plants and animals.

However, melted ice is not salty. So, this water sits at the surface and does not sink. This freshwater from glaciers and ice sheets is slowing down the ocean currents.

NOR
AMER

Pacific Ocean

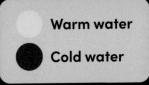
Warm water
Cold water

Ocean Currents

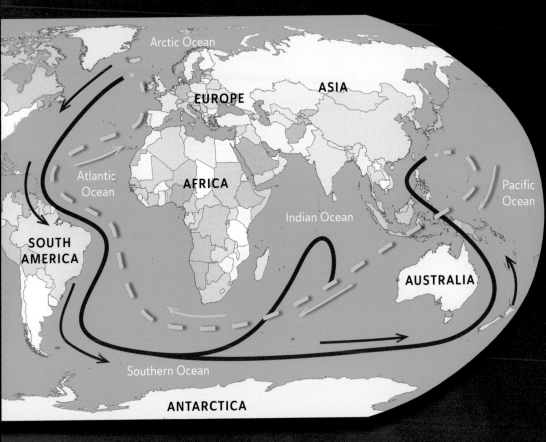

Arctic Ocean

EUROPE

ASIA

Atlantic Ocean

AFRICA

Pacific Ocean

Indian Ocean

SOUTH AMERICA

AUSTRALIA

Southern Ocean

ANTARCTICA

Some scientists think if enough polar ice melts, the ocean currents may even stop completely. If the Atlantic current stopped carrying its warmth to Europe, average temperatures there would fall by 9 to 18 degrees Fahrenheit (5 to 10 degrees Celsius).

Animals on Thin Ice

People living near coastlines are already seeing the effects of melting ice—and so are animals. Walruses and seals use sea ice for shelter and as places to raise their young. They feed on fish that live under and near the ice. As the ice disappears, so does their food source, and the animals are forced onto land. There, they can be attacked by **predators**.

Polar bears use sea ice, too. They stop on ice to rest while traveling through the ocean waters. The ice is also where they go for **mating**. Their main food source are ringed seals that also live on sea ice. With sea ice disappearing, polar bears may become **extinct** by 2100.

Even animals far from the Arctic are affected by melting ice. Many animals that live near the shore all over the world are seeing their homes and nests being flooded by rising seas.

What Are We Doing about It?

Global warming and melting ice can seem like problems too huge to fix. But experts are working to save glaciers. Some plan to drill in the hard rock under glaciers and fill these new holes with a cold, salty mixture that will freeze and strengthen the glaciers, keeping them in place. Others suggest making **artificial** icebergs and glaciers by collecting meltwater, refreezing it, and forming it into huge blocks.

This kind of creative thinking and problem-solving will not only help us save the world's ice. It will also help us stop global warming and protect the health of our planet!

Some **engineers** want to build a massive underwater wall around Antarctica's Thwaites Glacier to block the warm ocean water that is melting it. The 31-mile (50-km) wall could protect the glacier for up to 400 years!

Battle Melting Ice!

There's a lot we can do to help slow the melting of polar ice and fight the climate change that is causing it. The biggest impact comes when we use fewer fossil fuels. But that's not all. How can we battle melting ice?

Save electricity by turning off lights, computers, and devices when you're done with them. Unplug power cords and chargers when devices are not in use.

Reduce, reuse, recycle! The more paper, metal, and glass you reuse or recycle, the fewer fossil fuels have to be used to make new materials.

Plant trees! They suck up carbon dioxide and release oxygen for us to breathe. They can also help slow and soak up floodwaters along coastlines.

Support groups fighting to protect polar wildlife and preserve the Arctic and Antarctic. Follow them on social media, and donate money if you can.

Learn about alternative energy options and write to your local, state, and national representatives asking for their support of green energy.

Glossary

absorb to take in or soak up

artificial made by people instead of by nature

atmosphere layers of gases that surround Earth

carbon dioxide a gas given off when fossil fuels are burned

climate the typical weather in a place

currents movements of water in an ocean or river

engineers people who are trained to design and build things to solve problems

erode to wear away rocks, soil, or sand by natural forces such the movement of water and wind

extinct no longer existing

fossil fuels fuels such as coal, oil, and gas made from the remains of plants and other organisms that died millions of years ago

frigid very cold

glaciers huge areas of ice and snow found on mountains and near the North and South Poles

high tide when seawater is at its highest level and comes farthest up on land

ice sheets very large and thick areas of ice that form on level land and cover entire regions

mating coming together to have young

meltwater water that comes from the melting of ice and snow

predators animals that hunt and eat other animals

sea levels the average heights of the sea's surface

Read More

Haelle, Tara. *Melting Glaciers, Rising Seas (Taking Earth's Temperature).* Vero Beach, FL: Rourke Educational Media, 2019.

Haines, Serena. *Saving the Arctic.* Huntington Beach, CA: Teacher Created Materials, 2019.

Sneideman, Joshua, and Erin Twamley. *Climate Change: The Science behind Melting Glaciers and Warming Oceans with Hands-On Science Activities (Build It Yourself).* White River Junction, VT: Nomad Press, 2020.

Learn More Online

1. Go to **www.factsurfer.com** or scan the QR code below.

2. Enter "**Melting Ice**" into the search box.

3. Click on the cover of this book to see a list of websites.

Index

About the Author

Raymond Bergin is a writer living in New Jersey, where rising seas, increasingly powerful Atlantic storms, and regular flooding are beginning to change and erode the coastline and barrier islands. One of the ways he is fighting climate change is by trying not to use his air conditioner, even on the hottest, most humid New Jersey summer days.